# Grammar Made Easy

# for Infants

## Books 1 and 2

By

## C .M. Greenidge

First edition 2022:
Books 1 and 2 Combined and Revised

Cover design by Cheryl M Greenidge
Edited by E. Jerome Davis
Published by Cheryl .M. Greenidge

**ISBN:** 9798846385245

# Introduction

"Grammar Made Easy for Infants Books 1 and 2" introduces the concepts of **a** and **an**, **nouns, singular** and **plural**, and **capital letters, opposites**; **homophones**; **compound words**; **synonyms**; **capitalizing I**; the **full stop**; the **question mark**; joining sentences with '**but**' and '**and**'; the verbs, **am, is** and **are, has, have, was, were**, identifying **verbs** and **adjectives**.

Every effort has been made to present the concepts in a simple but interesting manner. The many activities are presented in a variety of ways in order to reinforce the concepts.

A feature of the text is the inclusion of Barbadian references which help to create that connection between child and activity.

"Grammar Made Easy for Infants Books 1 and 2" although specially designed for the 5 – 7 age group, may be helpful to older children who have not mastered the concepts presented.

# Section 1

## Vowels

- a and an

## Nouns

- things
- animals
- persons
- places

✤ Write the missing letter for the pictures.

a, e, i, o, u

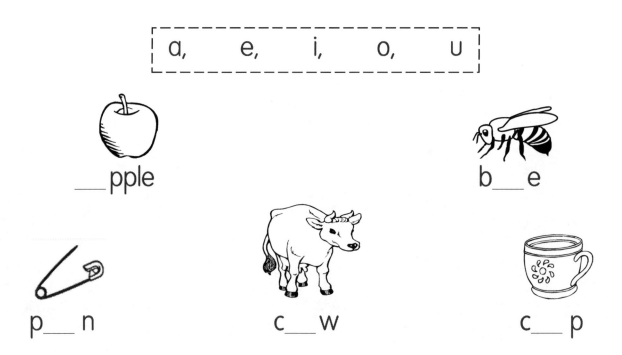

___pple

b___e

p___n

c___w

c___p

✤ The letters a, e, i, o, u are called vowels.
Circle the vowels in the clouds.

e d a z o

n u g e f

i v p u r

k a i t o

✿ Circle the words which begin with a vowel.

dog      igloo      van      sun      uncle

apple      pig      orange      bun

egg      chair      aunt

✿ Now write the words which you circled in the 'an' box. Write the other words in the 'a' box.

| an |
| --- |
| _____ |
| _____ |
| _____ |
| _____ |
| _____ |
| _____ |

| a |
| --- |
| _____ |
| _____ |
| _____ |
| _____ |
| _____ |

✿ We write 'an' before most words which begin with a vowel. Write 'an' before the words below.

_____ egg

_____ owl

_____ uncle

_____ oven

_____ apple

_____ ice cream

_____ ankle

_____ ear

_____ umbrella

✿ We write 'a' before most words which do not begin with a vowel. Write 'a' before the words below.

_____ cat

_____ wall

_____ flag

_____ ship

_____ ball

_____ tree

4

✿ Circle the correct word in the brackets.

( a     an ) house                    ( a     an ) insect

( a     an ) oven                      ( a     an ) ackee

( a     an ) earring                   ( a     an ) duck

✿ Circle the correct word in the brackets.

1. He has ( a     an ) bat.

2. That is ( a     an ) ugly picture.

3. May I have ( a     an ) snack?

4. We saw ( a     an ) ape at the zoo.

5. Barbados is ( a     an ) island.

5

✿ **Write 'a' or 'an' before these words.**

_____ book      _____ orange      _____ door

_____ eye      _____ aunt      _____ pencil

_____ mat      _____ rubber      _____ octopus

✿ **Write 'a' or 'an' in the spaces.**

1. He has _____ bat.

2. Did you see _____ alligator in the water?

3. I will buy _____ ice cream.

4. Have _____ good day.

5. She ate _____ apple and _____ banana.

6

✿ Write the naming words for these things.

pan       sun       net       pot       fire
bat       well       jet       banana

_____

_____

_____

_____

_____

_____

_____

_____

_____

✿ Words which name things are called naming words or nouns. Circle the noun in each box.

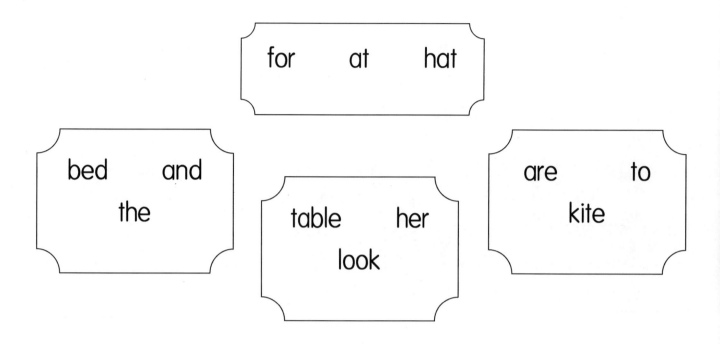

for    at    hat

bed    and
    the

table    her
    look

are    to
    kite

✿ In the sentences, circle the nouns which name <u>things</u>.

1. Look at the little box.

2. The car is red.

3. Here is my book.

4. Run to the tree.

5. She has a big bag.

6. This ball is mine.

✽ Write the nouns ( things ) below in suitable cans.

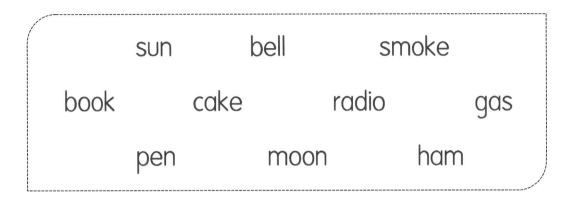

sun      bell      smoke

book      cake      radio      gas

pen      moon      ham

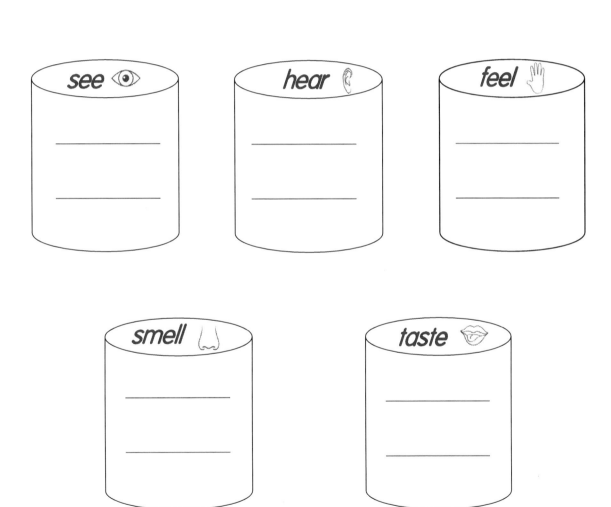

*see*     *hear*     *feel*

*smell*     *taste*

✿ Words which name animals are called naming words or nouns. Write the names of these animals.

| fish | pig | goat | duck |

_____    _____    _____    _____

✿ Write these nouns ( animals ) in the correct boxes.

| cat | bird | swan | eel | hen |
| whale | sheep | dog | shark |

| Live in the Sea | Can Fly | Have Four Legs |

_____

_____

_____

_____

_____

_____

_____

_____

_____

❀ **Circle the naming word ( noun ) in each box.**

| | | |
|---|---|---|
| write | bird | put |

| | | |
|---|---|---|
| fox | my | this |

| | | |
|---|---|---|
| come | all | bear |

| | | |
|---|---|---|
| chick | it | see |

| | | |
|---|---|---|
| for | ant | look |

❀ **In the sentences, circle the nouns which name animals.**

1. Look at the little rabbit.
2. The monkey is swinging.
3. Did you see my cat?
4. The cow is brown.
5. She has a big dog.

✿ Words which name persons are called naming words or nouns. Write the names of these persons.

| teacher | boy | daddy | police |

_____   _____   _____   _____

✿ Write these nouns ( persons ) in the correct boxes.

| boy | mummy | girl | daddy | baby | grandma |

adult

_____

_____

_____

child

_____

_____

_____

✿ **Circle the naming word ( noun ) in each box.**

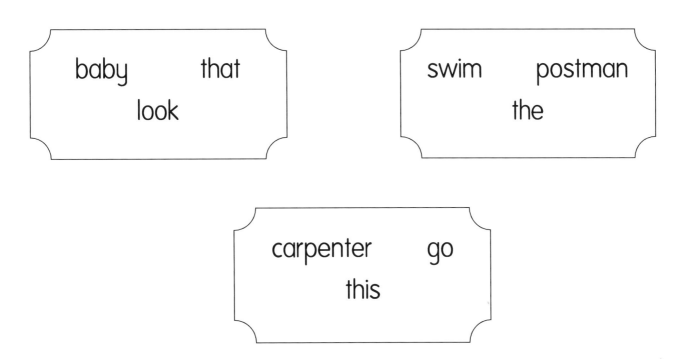

| | |
|---|---|
| baby      that<br>look | swim      postman<br>the |

carpenter     go
this

✿ **In the sentences, circle the nouns which name <u>persons</u>.**

1. The boys are playing.

2. The maid is cleaning.

3. Is he your granddad?

4. The chef is cooking.

5. Are the girls washing?

✤ Words which name places are called naming words or nouns. Write the names of these places.

| bathroom | mall | garden | park |

_____   _____   _____   _____

✤ Circle the noun ( place ) in each box.

| shop | the | talk |
| --- | --- | --- |

| school | of | then |
| --- | --- | --- |

| play | in | Bridgetown |
| --- | --- | --- |

| here | library | jump |
| --- | --- | --- |

| are | home | did |
| --- | --- | --- |

14

# ❀ Complete each sentence with the correct noun.

beach

bedroom

supermarket

church

office

1. The baby sleeps in the _____.

2. Daddy works in an _____.

3. The children play on the _____.

4. Mummy shops at the _____.

5. Grandma likes going to _____.

✿ Words which name animals, persons, places and things are called nouns. Write these nouns in the correct boxes.

| | | | | | |
|---|---|---|---|---|---|
| daddy | market | town | goat | runner | tablet |
| flower | chip | park | lizard | fly | driver |

Animal
_____
_____
_____

Person
_____
_____
_____

Place
_____
_____
_____

Thing
_____
_____
_____

❀ **Circle the nouns in the sentences.**

**Example:**   The (cat) is fat.

1. My cup is little.

2. Look at the tree.

3. The girl is going to school.

4. Is the beach far away?

5. A bird is on the wall.

6. An apple is on the table.

7. My book is in my bag.

8. Some children are on the pasture.

9. Water is in the well.

# Section 2

## Plurals

- most nouns
- nouns ending in 'ch'
- nouns ending in 'sh'
- nouns ending in 's'
- nouns ending in 'ss'
- nouns ending in 'x'
- irregular nouns

18

✿ We add 's' to most nouns to make them more than one. Make these nouns more than one.

| dog | ball | car |
|-----|------|-----|

dogs

| girl | mill | tree |
|------|------|------|

| cow | boat | chair |
|-----|------|-------|

❀ **Make these nouns more than one.**

rat

bird

cup

_____     _____     _____

❀ **Make the noun in brackets more than one.**
**Write it in the space.**

1. The boy eats two _____. ( bun )

2. The hen has many _____. ( egg )

3. Do you have the _____? ( ball )

4. Mummy buys some _____. ( pill )

5. Some _____ are in the pen. ( pig )

✿ Read the words for the pictures. Circle the letters that make the words similar.

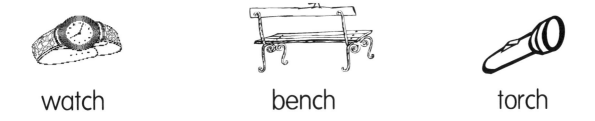

watch                   bench                   torch

✿ Underline the nouns which end with 'ch'. Then write them in the box.

| match | hook | latch | table | beach |
| cheese | torch | boat | church | chair |
| branch | shoe | peach | road | ostrich |

_____          _____

_____          _____

_____          _____

_____          _____

❀ We add 'es' to nouns which end with 'ch' to make them more than one. Make these nouns more than one.

| ostrich |
|---|

| peach |
|---|

| match |
|---|

_____        _____        _____

❀ Make these nouns more than one.

| One | More Than One |
|---|---|
| latch | _____ |
| torch | _____ |
| stitch | _____ |
| hutch | _____ |
| bunch | _____ |
| cockroach | _____ |

✿ Make these nouns more than one.

branch

church

sandwich

_____

_____

_____

✿ Make the noun in brackets more than one.
Write it in the space.

1. Do not play with _____. ( match )

2. Will you pack the _____? ( lunch )

3. The _____ are new. ( watch )

4. The man walks with _____. ( crutch )

5. We sat on the _____. ( bench )

✤ We add 'es' to nouns which end with 'sh' to make them more than one. Make these nouns more than one.

| dish | eyelash | flash |

_____       _____       _____

✤ Make these nouns more than one.

| One | More Than One |
|-----|---------------|
| lash | _____ |
| splash | _____ |
| wish | _____ |
| dash | _____ |
| crash | _____ |

✤ Make these nouns more than one.

| sash | toothbrush | fish |

_____    _____    _____

✤ Make the noun in brackets more than one.
Write it in the space.

1. Put the _____ in the sink. ( dish )

2. Mummy bought two _____. ( brush )

3. We saw many _____ in the sky. ( flash )

4. Her _____ are long. ( eyelash )

5. Did he hit the ball into the _____? ( bush )

❀ **Make the nouns more than one and write them in the correct boxes.**

| | | | | | |
|---|---|---|---|---|---|
| bed | kite | lash | table | bench | fish |
| car | marble | brush | chair | torch | church |

Add 's'

______________________

______________________

______________________

______________________

______________________

______________________

Add 'es'

______________________

______________________

______________________

______________________

______________________

______________________

✿ Make these nouns more than one.

chair s        flash___        house___        peach___

wish___        beach___        crash___        clock___

✿ Make the noun in brackets one. Write it in the space.

1. The _____ is on the table. ( cakes )

2. Daddy caught a _____ . ( fishes )

3. A _____ is in the sea. ( boats )

4. The man pulls the _____ . ( nets )

5. Did you wash the _____ ? ( dishes )

27

✾ **Make the noun in brackets more than one. Write it in the space.**

1. May I have my _____? ( pencil )

2. The girls put on their_____. ( sash )

3. Here are the _____. ( book )

4. Did he find the ball in the _____? bush )

5. The _____ were lit. ( torch )

6. The rabbits are in the _____. ( hutch )

7. Some _____ live in the tree. ( bird )

8. The West Indies won two _____? ( match )

9. Daddy has new paint _____. ( brush )

✿ We add 'es' to nouns which end with 's' or 'ss' to make them more than one. Make these nouns more than one.

lens

bus

atlas

dress

cross

class

princess

walrus

glass

✿ **Make the noun in brackets more than one. Write it in the space.**

1. I have two new _____ ( dress ).

2. The _____ are going to Bridgetown. ( bus )

3. I gave daddy many _____. ( kiss )

4. Did she break the _____? ( glass )

5. Look for the _____ in the cupboard. ( lens )

✿ **Make the noun in brackets one. Write it in the space.**

1. She is a pretty _____. ( princesses )

2. Are the boys in the _____? ( classes )

3. That _____ came from Farley Hill. ( buses )

4. A _____ is on the church. ( crosses )

❀ We add 'es' to most nouns which end with 'x' to make them more than one. Make these nouns more than one.

| sax | fox | box |
|-----|-----|-----|

_____    _____    _____

❀ Make these nouns more than one.

| One | More Than One |
|-----|---------------|
| six | _____ |
| box | _____ |
| fax | _____ |
| mix | _____ |
| wax | _____ |

✤ **Make the noun in the brackets more than one.**
  **Write it in the space.**

1. Mummy paid her _____. ( tax )

2. The men will paint the _____. ( box )

3. Many _____ were in the den. ( fox )

4. Sobers hit six _____ in one over. ( six )

✤ **Make the noun in the brackets one.**
  **Write it in the space.**

1. Five plus one makes _____. ( sixes )

2. She has one _____. ( boxes )

3. The _____ ate the hen. ( foxes )

4. Daddy pays road _____. ( taxes )

✿ Make the nouns more than one and write them in the correct boxes.

| | | | | | |
|---|---|---|---|---|---|
| door | house | box | road | lens | cross |
| van | tablet | boss | cake | atlas | pox |

Add 's'

_____

_____

_____

_____

_____

_____

Add 'es'

_____

_____

_____

_____

_____

_____

✿ **Some nouns change to become many ( more than one ). Write the correct noun in each space.**

| children    feet    mice    geese    men |
| --- |

**One**                                          **Many**

foot                                    _____

man                                     _____

child                                   _____

mouse                                   _____

goose                                   _____

✽ Here are more nouns which change to become many. Write the correct noun in each space.

| teeth | women | oxen | dice |
|-------|-------|------|------|

**One**                           **Many**

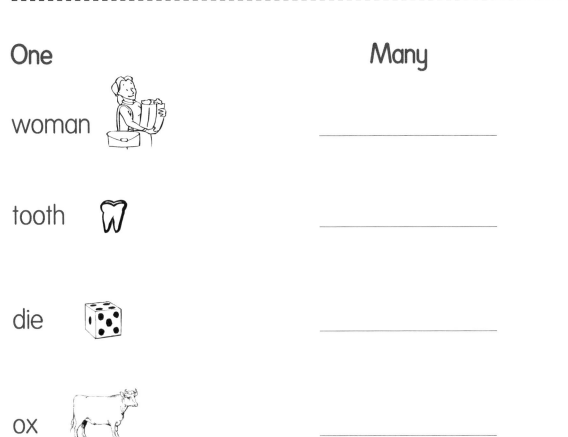

woman

tooth

die

ox

_____

_____

_____

_____

✽ These nouns do not change. Make them many.

sheep

_____

deer

_____

❀ **Make the nouns more than one. Write them in the correct spaces.**

| | | | | |
|---|---|---|---|---|
| foot | woman | man | sheep | |
| goose | child | tooth | die | mouse |

____________  ____________  ____________

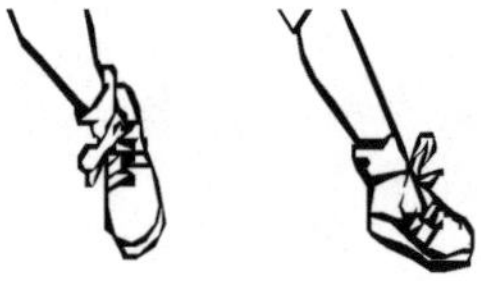

____________  ____________  ____________

____________  ____________  ____________

✿ **Make the noun in brackets more than one.**
**Write it in the space.**

1. The _____ are digging a well. ( man )

2. Are the _____ on the pasture? ( sheep )

3. The _____ were in the garden. ( woman )

4. She got her _____ cleaned today. ( tooth )

5. Many _____ are in the cupboard.( mouse )

6. Some _____ are in the classroom. ( child )

7. Her _____ were broken. ( foot )

8. They were playing with _____. ( die )

✿ **Make the noun in brackets one. Write it in the space.**

1. The _____ buys a breadfruit. ( women )

2. My _____ has come out. ( teeth )

3. A _____ is in the boat ( men )

4. The _____ plays with the toy. ( children )

5. A _____ is a cube. ( dice )

6. Her _____ is hurting. ( feet )

7. A _____ is in the hole. ( mice )

8. The _____ is eating grass. ( sheep )

✿ Make the nouns many. Write them in the correct spaces.

> glass     tree     match     deer
> box     fish     book     lens     chair

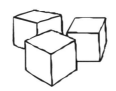

_____     _____     _____

_____     _____     _____

_____     _____     _____

✿ **Make the nouns many and write them in the correct boxes.**

door      fox      foot      tooth      road      dish

church      truck      man      cane      mouse      gas

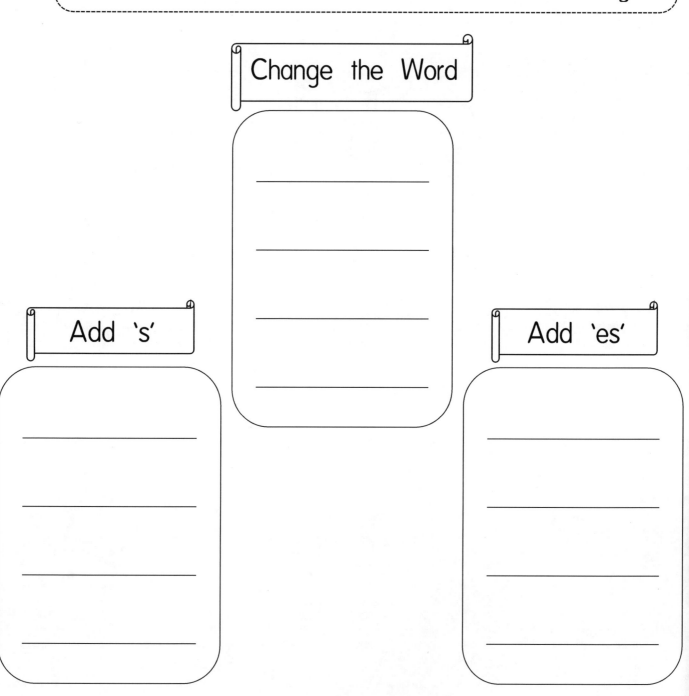

Change the Word

Add 's'

Add 'es'

40

# Section 3

## Capital Letters

- Capitalizing the letter i
- days of the week
- months of the year
- names of persons
- names of places
- names of animals
- special names

✿ **Match the common letter to the capital letter.**

a       e       g       r       n       l

G       N       A       L       E       R

✿ **Write the capital letters for these common letters.**

b _____    d _____    f _____    h _____

i _____    j _____    k _____    m _____

p _____    q _____    t _____    y _____

✿ **Write these words in capital letters.**

come          down          this

_____   _____   _____

✿ The word 'I' is always written with a capital letter. Write a capital 'I' in each space.

.1. _____ am six years old.

2. _____ have two sisters.

3. Where did _____ put my pencil?

4. _____ do my homework before _____ watch T.V.

✿ Write these sentences correctly.

1. i am not well.

_____

2. i went to Rhianna's concert.

_____

3. When i go to church, i pray.

_____

❀ The days of the week always begin with a capital letter. Write these days correctly.

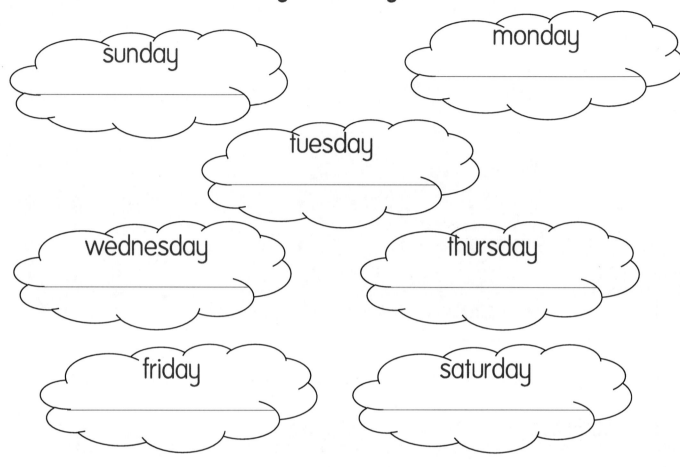

sunday

monday

tuesday

wednesday

thursday

friday

saturday

❀ Write these sentences correctly.

1. She went to church on sunday.

_____

2. Can we go to the beach on friday?

_____

❁ The table shows fruits which some children ate.
Complete the sentences with the days written correctly.

| monday | tuesday | wednesday | thursday | friday |
|--------|---------|-----------|----------|--------|
| | | | | |
| mango | tamarinds | watermelon | tomatoes | fig |

1. Tom ate tomatoes on _____.

2. Mia had a mango on _____.

3. On _____ Fred ate a fig.

4. On _____ Tammy ate tamarinds.

5. Wendy had watermelon on _____.

✿ The months of the year always begin with a capital letter. Write these months of the year correctly.

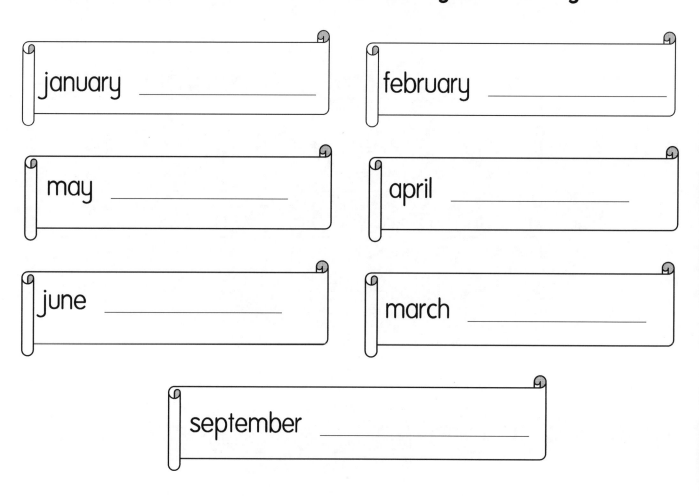

january _____

february _____

may _____

april _____

june _____

march _____

september _____

✿ Write these sentences correctly.

1. My holiday is in july and august.

_____

2. Is her birthday in december?

_____

❀ **Write the names of the months correctly in the spaces.**

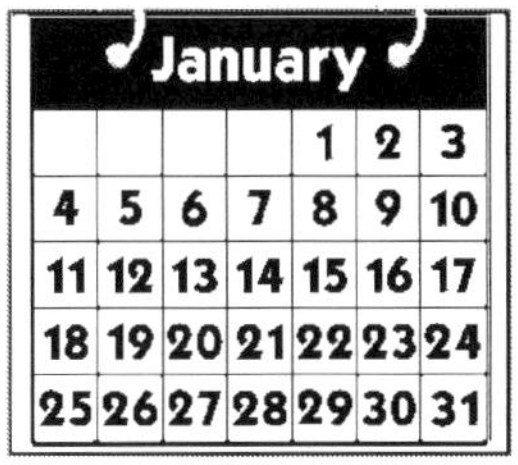
January
1 2 3
4 5 6 7 8 9 10
11 12 13 14 15 16 17
18 19 20 21 22 23 24
25 26 27 28 29 30 31

1. Christmas Day is in ____________________.

   december

2. ____________________ is the first month of the year.

   january

3. Kadooment day is in ____________________.

   august

4. ____________________ 30th is Independence Day.

   november

5. National Heroes Day is in ____________________.

   april

6. The first of ____________________ is called Labour Day.

   may

✿ Always begin the names of persons with a capital letter. Copy the names of these girls correctly.

jada  callender

_____

danielle  gibson

_____

✿ Complete these sentences.

1. My name is _____

2. My friend's name is _____

3. My teacher's name is _____

4. My games teacher is _____

✿ The table shows things which some children like doing. Complete the sentences with the names written correctly.

| cooking | cricket | swimming | football | riding |
|---------|---------|----------|----------|--------|
| | | | | |
| rhea | joshua | ashlee | nicoli | tiffany |

1. _____ likes playing cricket.

2. _____ enjoys playing football.

3. _____ likes swimming.

4. _____ likes to ride her bicycle.

5. _____ enjoys cooking.

❀ The names of places always begin with a capital letter. Write the missing capital letters for the parishes on the map of Barbados.

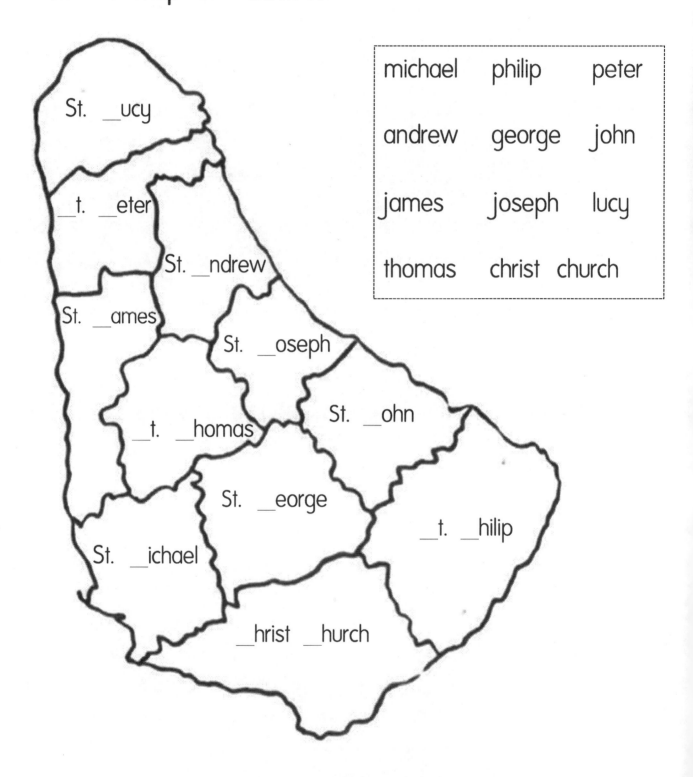

St. __ucy

__t. __eter

St. __ndrew

St. __ames

St. __oseph

__t. __homas

St. __ohn

St. __eorge

__t. __hilip

St. __ichael

__hrist __hurch

| michael | philip | peter |
| andrew | george | john |
| james | joseph | lucy |
| thomas | christ | church |

✿ Special names of places always begin with capital letters. Write these sentences correctly.

1. They went to *oistins* and *bridgetown*.

_____

2. Daddy will take us to *bushy park*.

_____

3. Are they going to *dominica* ?

_____

4. **harrison's** cave is in **st. thomas**.

_____


✿ **Complete these sentences.**

1. My school is in _____

_____

2. I live in _____

_____

51

✿ Special names of pets always begin with capital letters.

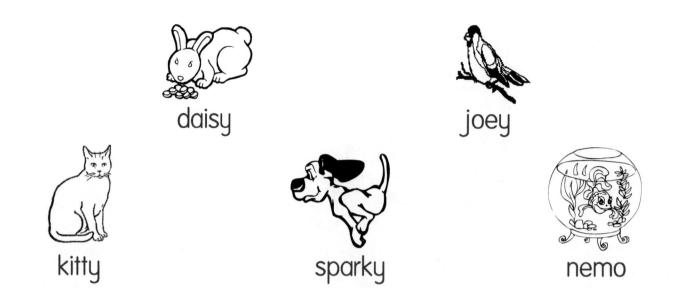

daisy

joey

kitty

sparky

nemo

✿ Complete the sentences with the names written correctly.

1. The fish is _____.

2. The cat is _____.

3. The bird is called _____.

4. The name of the dog is _____.

5. _____ is the rabbit.

❀ **Special names of things always begin with capital letters.**

toyota

samsung

nike

barbie

bico

❀ **Complete the sentences with the names written correctly.**

1. She has a ____________________ doll.

2. Daddy drives a ____________________ car.

3. My cellphone is a ____________________.

4. I like to eat ____________________ ice cream.

5. He wears ____________________ shoes.

✻ Write these special names correctly.

miss browne

_____

dr. pinder

_____

mr. edey

_____

monday

_____

tuesday

_____

saturday

_____

chefette

_____

casa grande

_____

sheraton

_____

july

_____

august

_____

october

_____

❀ **Write these sentences correctly.**

1. My cat's name is frisky.

_____

2. She will be six on monday.

_____

3. My uncle's birthday is in april.

_____

4. Does your daddy drive a toyota car?

_____

5. They live in st. michael.

_____

7. i sat beside roshanna turney.

_____

# Section 4

- Opposites
- Homophones
- Compound words
- Synonyms

✸ Write the words and their opposites under the correct pictures.

in out      big little      wet dry

on off      up down

_____  _____  _____  _____

_____  _____

  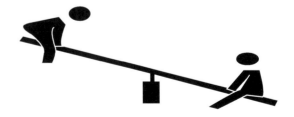

_____  _____  _____  _____

✿ Write the words and their opposites under the correct pictures.

```
push  pull        open  closed      happy  sad
         hot  cold         full  empty
```

_____   _____        _____   _____

_____        _____

_____   _____        _____   _____

✤ In the brackets, underline the opposite of the word in bold.

Example: The mouse ran **down** the clock.
( under   <u>up</u>   in )

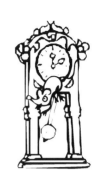

1. The bag was **full**.   ( fill   empty   fell )

2. Did you **close** the window? ( shut   over   open )

3. My ball is **little**. ( bin   small   big )

4. Did she get **in** the bus? ( on   out   over )

5. Turn on the **hot** water tap. ( cold   cot   hold )

6. The boy got **on** his bike. ( front   off   for )

7. You need to **push** the gate to get out.
( open   pill   pull )

✿ **Write the opposite of each underlined word.**

1. Fire is _____ but ice cream is <u>cold.</u>

2. This duck is <u>dry</u> but that one is _____.

3. The boy was _____ the float now he is <u>out.</u>

4. A see-saw goes _____ and <u>down.</u>

5. The girl is <u>happy</u> but the boy is _____.

6. A mouse is <u>little</u> but an elephant is _____.

✿ **The pictures show opposites. Write the word for each.**

right  wrong  left     short  tall  long     old  new  young

_____  _____     _____  _____

2+3=5 ✓    2+3=4 ✗

_____  _____     _____  _____

_____  _____     _____  _____

## ✿ Write the opposite of the underlined word.

1. My sums were <u>right</u> but yours were _____.

2. Did you look <u>left</u> and _____?

3. His kite has a _____ tail and <u>long</u> cord.

4. Mark is <u>short</u> but Mia is _____.

5. Granddad is <u>old</u> but my baby sister is _____.

6. Take the <u>new</u> book from the box and leave the _____ one.

✿ Complete the puzzle below with words from the box to show opposites for the pictures.

| day | laugh | stand | light | hard | dull |

1    sit

2    soft

3    night

4    heavy

5    sharp

6    cry

1 ▢▢▢▢▢

2 ▢▢▢▢

3 ▢▢▢

4 ▢▢▢▢▢

5 ▢▢▢▢

6 ▢▢▢▢▢

✿ In each box, circle the two words that are opposite and write them on the lines.

| good | bad |
| --- | --- |
| dad | goal |

_____

_____

| over | class |
| --- | --- |
| oven | under |

_____

_____

| but | top |
| --- | --- |
| stop | bottom |

_____

_____

| front | bark |
| --- | --- |
| from | back |

_____

_____

| fast | first |
| --- | --- |
| slow | fist |

_____

_____

| cover | form |
| --- | --- |
| clean | dirty |

_____

_____

✿ Homophones are words that sound alike but are spelt differently and have different meanings.
Circle the correct word for each picture.

✿ Circle the correct word from the brackets to complete each sentence.

1. We ( see    sea ) with our eyes.

2. Mother bakes cakes with ( flour    flower ).

3. I have a new ( pair    pear ) of shoes.

4. Will you ( be    bee ) my friend?

5. Can we go ( two    to ) the fair?

6. That mango tree is ( bear    bare ).

✿ **Circle the correct word for each picture.**

won

one

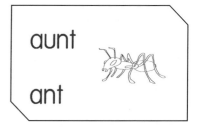

eight

ate

8

aunt

ant

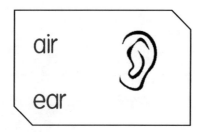

sun

son

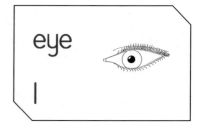

air

ear

eye

I

✿ **Circle the correct word from the brackets to complete each sentence.**

1. ( Won    One ) cup is in the sink.

2. She    ( ate    eight ) one sugar apple.

3. ( Ant    Aunt ) Jan is cooking.

4. Mr. Jones has one ( sun    son ).

5. The ( air    ear ) from the fan is cool.

6. ( I    Eye ) am six years old.

66

## ✿ Write the word for the picture.

hair, hare      sail, sale      dear, deer

some, sum     pail, pale     meat, meet

cell, sell      tail, tale      ball, bawl

_____    _____    _____

$4 + 2 = 6$

_____    _____    _____

_____    _____    _____

❀ **Circle the correct word in the brackets.**

1. Please for ( some    sum ) ice cream.

2. Do they ( cell    sell ) pizza on Fridays?

3. Her ( hear    hair    hare ) is very long.

4. Road tennis is played with a small ( ball    bawl ).

5. Shall we go to ( meat    meet ) mother?

6. I like the ( tail    tale ) 'The Three Little Pigs'.

7. The sick girl looks ( pail    pale ).

8. That chain is very ( dear    deer    dare ).

9. Our school is having a cake ( sail    sale ).

✿ **Underline the correct word in the brackets.**

1. He ( won   one ) first prize.

2. I got all my sums ( write   right   rite ).

3. ( Ewe   You ) are my best friend.

4. We had fun at the ( fair   fare ).

5. We went shopping for ( close   clothes ).

6. She picked a ( flower   flour ) from the garden.

7. ( I   Eye ) love Chefette ice cream.

8. Did you put the ( meet   meat ) on the grill?

9. The postman brought the ( mail   male ).

10. I am going ( two   to   too ) the supermarket.

✿ Compound words are formed when we join two words. Read the words then write them together to make compound words.

1. rain + coat ___raincoat___

2. hand + bag _____

3. tooth + brush _____

4. sun + flower _____

5. shoe + lace _____

6. bed + room _____

7. ear + rings _____

8. dog + house _____

✿ Match these words to form compound words. Then write the word formed on the line.

grass             bug     ladybug

lady              fly

butter           bird

earth            hopper

black            bee

honey          worm

✿ **Match the words to form compound words. Then write the words formed on the lines.**

milk                    corn

_____

turn                    bread

_____

sweet                   shake

_____

pop                     melon

_____

coco                    over

_____

water                   nut

_____

# Match the words that have the same meaning.

big

shut

little

ill

happy

road

sick

small

large

street

closed

glad

❀ Words that have the same meaning are called synonyms. In each line, circle the synonym for the first word.

| | | | |
|---|---|---|---|
|  *thin* | tin | slim | fat |
|  *same* | begin | equal | star |
|  *fat* | stout | far | rat |
|  *gift* | give | lift | present |
|  *cut* | cute | slice | cure |
|  *fast* | quick | slow | fist |

# Section 5

## Punctuation

- Full stop
- Question mark

## Joining sentences with

- But
- And

✤ A capital letter is placed at the beginning of telling sentences. Copy these telling sentences and put a capital letter at the beginning.

1. it is a sunny day.

_____

2. the house is big.

_____

3. a garden is in front of the house.

_____

4. many pretty flowers are in the garden.

_____

❀ A full stop is placed at the end of telling sentences. Copy these telling sentences and put a full stop at the end of each.

1. We go on the pasture

_____

2. Our games teacher takes us

_____

3. The children have fun

_____

4. The bell rings for lunch

_____

5. We eat macaroni pie and chicken

_____

✿ **Copy these telling sentences and put in the capital letters and the full stops.**

1. she is little

_____

2. his bag is blue

_____

3. my cup is empty

_____

4. we will go to Miami Beach

_____

5. i like sweetbread

_____

6. the buses are going to Rock Hall

_____

7. the hare is a fast animal

_____

8. she lives in Bushy Park, St. Philip

_____

✿ The first word in each question about the picture is a question word. Circle it and write it in the box.

1. What is in the tree?

2. Why is the bird in the tree?

3. Which bird is in the tree?

4. Where is the blackbird?

5. How many birds are in the picture?

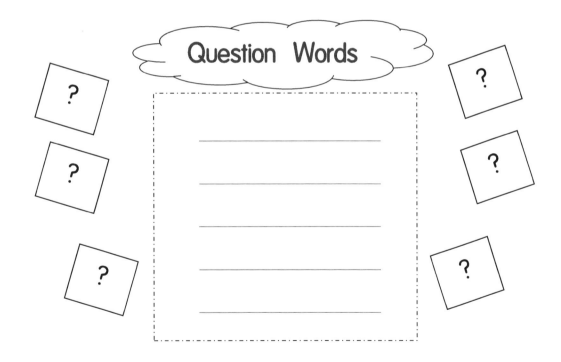

Question Words

?
?
?
?
?

❀ The first word in each question about the nursery rhyme below is a helping word.

> *Jack be nimble*
> *Jack be quick*
> *Jack jumped over the candle stick.*

❀ Circle the helping words and write them in the box.

1. Is Jack running quickly?
2. Was Jack holding the candle stick?
3. Did Jack jump over the candle stick?
4. Do you think the candle was lit?
5. Will Jack jump high or low?

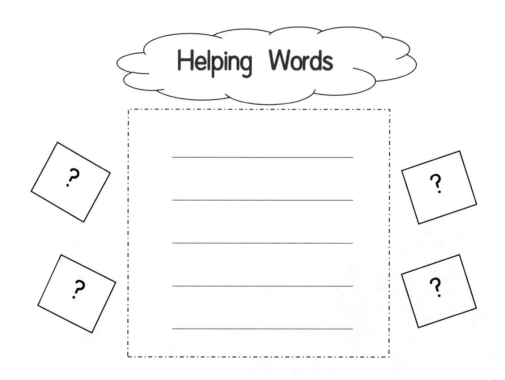

Helping Words

✿ Question words and helping words help us to ask questions. Choose a suitable question word or helping word for each space.

When

Are

1. _____ is your name?

Do

2. _____ old are you?

What

3. _____ is your birthday?

Why

4. _____ you going to the party?

How

5. _____ you have my book?

6. _____ is he crying?

❀ **A question mark is placed at the end of questions. Copy these questions and put a question mark at the end of each.**

1. Has he paid the bill

___

2. Can you swim

___

3. Where is Six Men's Bay

___

4. Did you win the race

___

5. Who won the netball game

___

6. Am I your friend

___

7. Were they at Folkstone Park

___

8. Why did you pick the flower

___

�֎ **Copy these sentences and write a question mark or a full stop at the end.**

1. He has gone home

_____

2. Where is Bussa Statue

_____

3. Did you eat my tamarind ball

_____

4. It is a big car

_____

5. When are you leaving

_____

6. Does he catch the bus to St. Lucy

_____

7. She is in Errol Barrow Park

_____

8. May I have a conkie

_____

✿ **Join the two sentences by replacing the full stop with 'but'.**

**Example:** He loves the sea. He cannot swim.

He loves the sea **but he** cannot swim.

1. He is tall. She is short.

_____

2. I can cook. My sister cannot cook.

_____

3. Jakobi is afraid of frogs. I am not.

_____

4. We went to the zoo. It was closed.

_____

5. He wanted to drive. The car would not start.

_____

✿ Join the two sentences by replacing the full stop and the repeated words with 'and'.

Example: I can read. I can write.

I can read **and** write.

1. I am short. I am fat.

_____

2. He has a bat. He has a ball.

_____

3. She likes to draw. She likes to colour.

_____

4. Look at the boy. Look at the girl.

_____

5. I have an apple. I have a pear.

_____

# Section 6

## Verbs

- Am, is and are
- Has and have
- Was and were
- Identifying verbs

✿ We use the word 'am' when we are speaking or writing about ourselves.

I

am

✿ Write 'am' in the spaces below.

1. I _____ five years old.

2. I _____ in Infants A.

3. I _____ happy to be at school today.

✿ Write 'am' in the spaces.

1. I _____ angry.

2. I _____ afraid.

3. I _____ sad.

✿ We use the word 'is' when we are speaking or writing about one thing, animal, person or place.

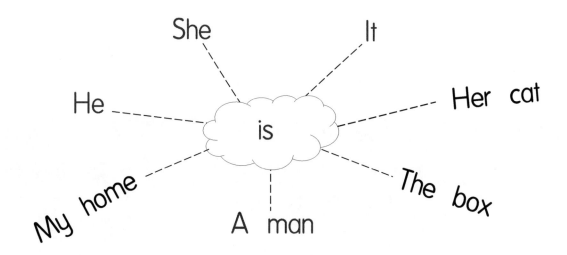

✿ Circle the words which mean one.

girl        birds        cars        wall        it

home        pigs        beds        he        tables

duck        man        she        dogs        hills

✿ Now write the words which you circled on the lines.

_____    _____    _____    _____

_____    _____    _____    _____

✤ In each sentence, circle the word or words we are speaking about. Then, write 'is' in the spaces.

Example: (The bird) is in the tree.

1. A jet _____ in the sky.

2. My book _____ red.

3. The man _____ pulling the net.

4. She _____ playing with her dolls.

5. Ken _____ flying his kite.

6. _____ it a big dog?

7. He _____ going to Three Houses Park.

8. It _____ raining.

❀ We use the word 'are' when we are speaking or writing about more than one thing, animal, person or place.

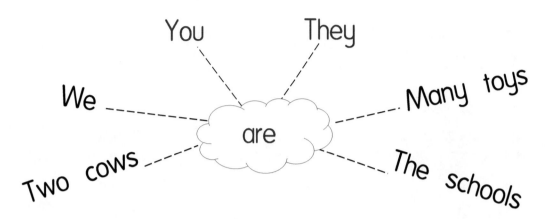

❀ Circle the words which mean more than one.

balls     tree     apple     we     boys

fan     pots     jet     eggs     mats

they     pen     boat     parks     bus

❀ Now write the words which you circled on the lines.

_____  _____  _____  _____

_____  _____  _____  _____

❀ **In each sentence, circle the word or words we are speaking about. Then, write 'are' in the spaces.**

**Example:** (The cups) are on the table.

1. My books __________ in my bag.

2. We __________ not going home.

3. The boys __________ picking dunks.

4. Ben and Joe __________ by the sea.

5. The buses __________ on the road.

6. __________ you going to the party?

7. They __________ in the nest.

8. Some men __________ fishing.

Complete the tables by putting 'am' 'is' or 'are' in the spaces. We always use the word 'are' with 'you'.

| | | | |
|---|---|---|---|
| I | | We | |
| He | | You ( one ) | |
| She | | You ( many ) | |
| It | | They | |
| A  boy | | The  girls | |
| My  eye | | Your  teeth | |
| His  book | | Her  brushes | |
| Each  child | | Some  boxes | |
| That  car | | Those  men | |

✿ Correctly match the boxes to the clouds.

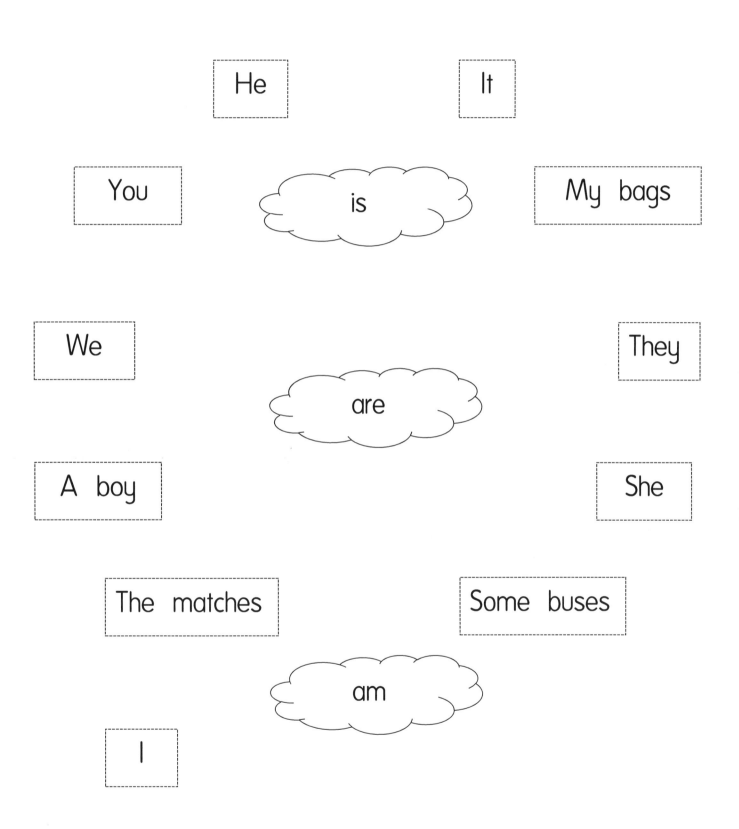

He

It

You

is

My bags

We

are

They

A boy

She

The matches

Some buses

am

I

✿ **Write 'is', 'are' or 'am' in the spaces below.**

1. A  bird _____ on  the  wall.

2. The  children _____ in  the  park.

3. I _____ not  well.

4. _____ it  raining?

5. He _____ playing  with  his  dog.

6. We _____ at  school.

7. _____ you  going  with  me?

8. She _____ cooking  cou-cou  and  flying  fish.

9. They _____ flying  their  kites.

10. The  dresses _____ pretty.

✿ We use the word 'has' when we are speaking or writing about one thing, animal, person or place.

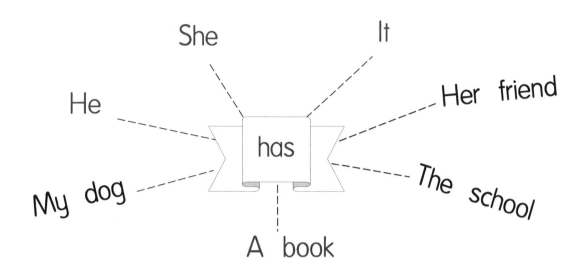

✿ Circle the words which mean one.

buses        sash        bake        boxes        beach

glass        she         chair       matches      vans

door         tables      it                   pears        clocks

✿ Now write the circled words on the lines.

_____  _____  _____  _____

_____  _____  _____  _____

95

✿ In each sentence, circle the word or words we are speaking about. Then, write 'has' in the spaces.

Example: ⟨A cat⟩ <u>has</u> whiskers.

1. The park _____ many trees.

2. My little sister _____ a skipping rope.

3. It _____ a long tail.

4. The car _____ big wheels.

5. _____ the girl eaten the bakes?

6. She _____ my pencil.

7. He _____ the same book.

8. My mummy _____ many friends.

✿ We use the word 'have' when we are speaking or writing about more than one thing, animal, person or place and with 'I' and 'you'.

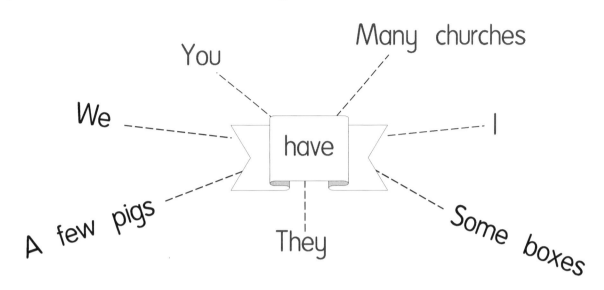

✿ Circle the words which mean more than one.

| | | | | |
|---|---|---|---|---|
| chair | fishes | cake | beach | foxes |
| they | trucks | match | bus | we |
| benches | door | glasses | tables | house |

✿ Now write the circled words on the lines.

_____  _____  _____  _____

_____  _____  _____  _____

✾ In each sentence, circle the word or words we are speaking about. Then, write 'have' in the spaces.

Example: ⟨Many children⟩ have pets.

1. You _____ to go to school.

2. Some schools _____ been closed.

3. We _____ won the cricket game.

4. _____ you seen the puppet show?

5. I _____ to see the tuk band.

6. They _____ not done their homework.

7. The men _____ lots of books.

8. _____ the tables been cleaned?

✿ Complete the tables by putting 'has' or 'have' in the spaces.

| | |
|---|---|
| He | |
| She | |
| It | |
| The plant | |
| My mp3 | |
| Her tablet | |
| Each boy | |
| My toe | |
| That office | |

| | |
|---|---|
| I | |
| We | |
| You ( one ) | |
| You ( many ) | |
| They | |
| The goats | |
| Your books | |
| Both girls | |
| Some parks | |

✿ **Correctly match the boxes to 'has' and 'have'.**

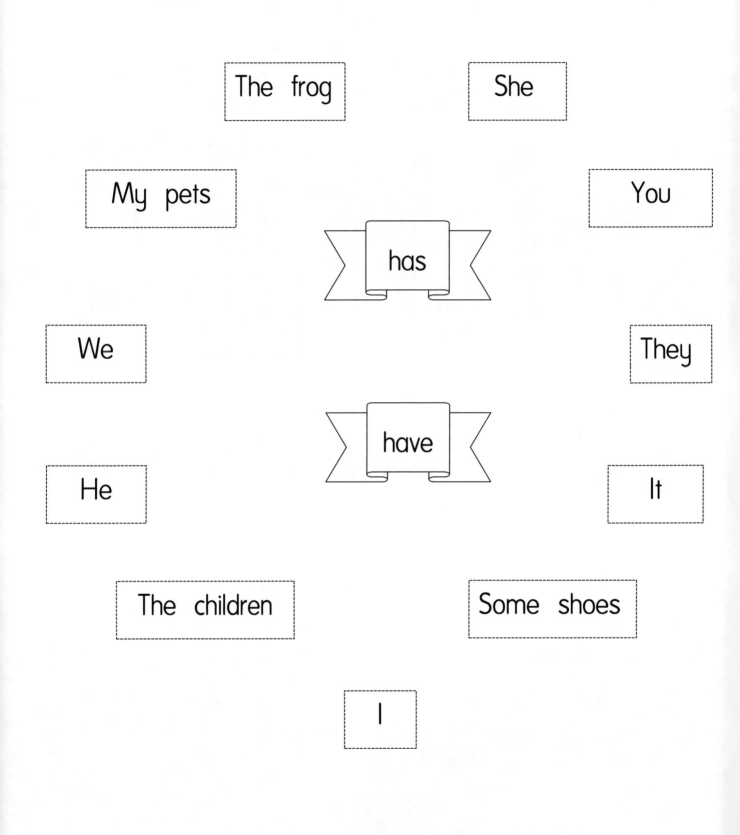

The frog

She

My pets

You

has

We

They

have

He

It

The children

Some shoes

I

✿ **Write has or have in the spaces below.**

1. They _____ to go to St. Mary's Church.

2. The girls _____ to catch the bus to St. James.

3. She _____ a cold.

4. Mother _____ cooked dumplings in the soup.

5. He _____ played cricket before.

6. Those women _____ worked at the Crane Hotel.

7. The cats _____ fleas.

8. The lemonade _____ to be strained.

9. Both of her feet _____ been broken.

10. Some schools _____ Cub Scouts.

✿ We use the word 'was' when we are speaking or writing about one thing, animal, person or place.

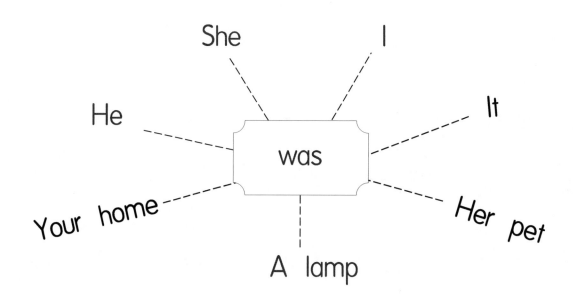

✿ Circle the words which mean one.

| | | | | |
|---|---|---|---|---|
| book | goats | she | pencil | boxes |
| fishes | cupcake | frogs | nail | it |
| mice | I | women | man | chairs |

✿ Now write the circled words on the lines.

_____  _____  _____  _____

_____  _____  _____  _____

✿ In each sentence, circle the word or words we are speaking about. Then, write 'was' in the spaces.

Example: (The cat) <u>was</u> climbing the tree.

1. I _____ going to the beach.

2. He _____ five years old yesterday.

3. She _____ happy to see me.

4. The mauby _____ on the table.

5. My brother _____ sick last week.

6. It _____ very sunny yesterday.

7. _____ she given a prize?

8. Joshua _____ crying because he had fallen.

❀ We use the word 'were' when we are speaking or writing about more than one thing, animal, person or place and always with you.

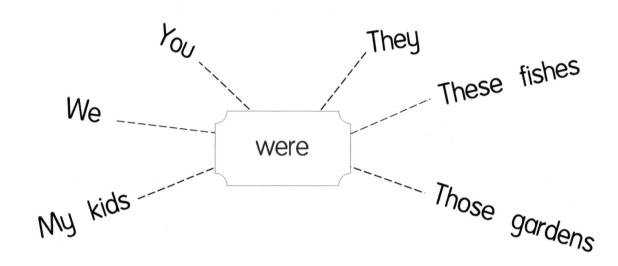

❀ Circle the words which mean more than one.

| | | | | |
|---|---|---|---|---|
| rubber | we | teeth | duck | churches |
| marble | okras | children | nail | oxen |
| woman | bucket | umbrella | they | tables |

❀ Now write the circled words on the lines.

_____   _____   _____   _____

_____   _____   _____   _____

✿ **In each sentence, circle the word or words we are speaking about. Then, write 'were' in the spaces.**

Example: (The sheep) <u>were</u> grazing on the pasture.

1. Some children _____ in the bathroom.

2. My cousins _____ singing a spouge song.

3. They _____ shopping on Swan Street.

4. Chad and David _____ racing.

5. We _____ eating ice cream at the fair.

6. The girls _____ playing hopscotch.

7. Two mice _____ on the trap.

8. _____ you in Queen's Park?

# Complete the tables by putting 'was' or 'were' in the spaces.

| | |
|---|---|
| He | |
| She | |
| It | |
| I | |
| His hand | |
| That lizard | |
| The town | |
| Our teacher | |
| This game | |

| | |
|---|---|
| We | |
| You ( one ) | |
| You ( many ) | |
| They | |
| Some nails | |
| The riders | |
| Their shoes | |
| Two houses | |
| Those ants | |

❀ Correctly match the boxes to 'was' and 'were'.

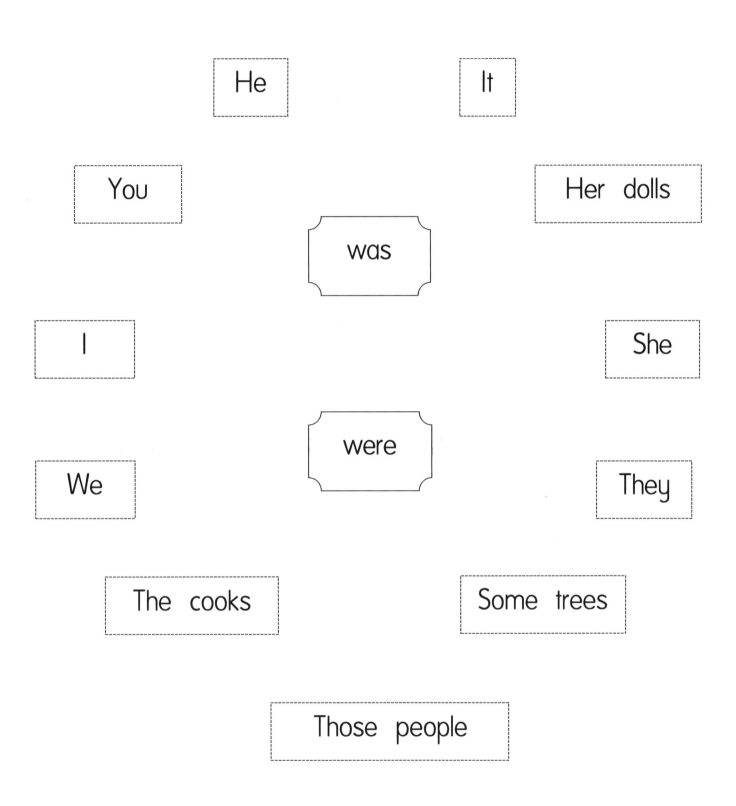

He

It

You

Her dolls

was

I

She

were

We

They

The cooks

Some trees

Those people

✤ **Write 'was' or 'were' in the spaces below.**

1. You _____ hopping like a bunny.

2. I _____ playing with my dog.

3. Those firemen _____ putting out the fire.

4. The children _____ watching C.B.C television.

5. Mother _____ cooking our lunch.

6. _____ they flying their kites at the Garrison?

7. It _____ a beautiful picture.

8. She _____ riding a pony at the fair.

9. We _____ sitting on the bench.

10. They _____ at Brandons Beach.

✿ Action words are called verbs. Write the verb for each picture on the line.

| swing | kick | bat | run | cook |
|---|---|---|---|---|
| play | jump | eat | sit | |

_____

_____

_____

_____

_____

_____

_____

_____

_____

❀ **Circle the verbs in the rhyme.**

> One, two, buckle my shoe;
>
> Three, four, shut the door;
>
> Five, six, pick up sticks;
>
> Seven, eight, lay them straight;
>
> Nine, ten, a big fat hen.

❀ **Circle the verb in each box.**

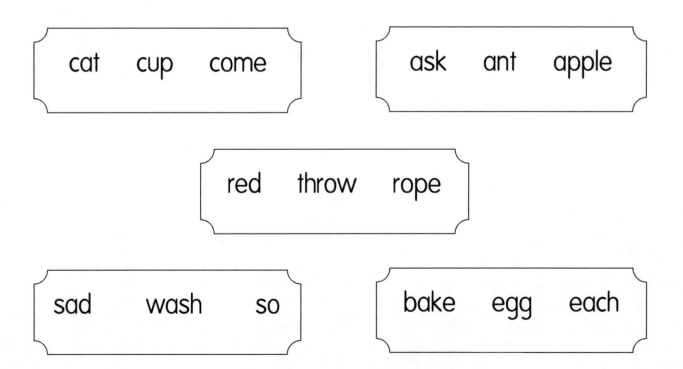

cat     cup     come

ask     ant     apple

red     throw     rope

sad     wash     so

bake     egg     each

110

✿ Circle the verb in each box.

day    at    copy

week    on    see

flower    the    play

✿ Choose suitable verbs to complete the sentences.

tie    comb    dress    play    fly

1. I can _____ my kite.

2. I can _____ my hair.

3. I can _____ my shoelaces.

4. I can _____ dominoes.

5. I can _____ myself.

✿ **Choose a verb to complete each sentence.**

riding        skipping        dancing

painting        drumming        singing

1. The  bear  is  _____.

2. The  monkey  is  _____.

3. Is  the  frog  _____?

4. The  dog  is  _____.

5. A  rat  is  _____.

6. Is  the  pig  _____?

✿ **Add 'ing' to these verbs.**

Example:  open  <u>open**ing**</u>

see  _____  draw  _____

talk  _____  read  _____

ask  _____  sleep  _____

think  _____  learn  _____

✿ **Add 'ing' to the verbs in brackets and write them in the spaces.**

1. Mother is _____ sea eggs. ( cook )

2. Were the men _____ the road? ( fix )

3. She was _____ mauby. ( drink )

4. The dogs were _____.  ( fight )

✿ We add 's' to many verbs when we are speaking or writing about one thing, animal, person or place to show action that is happening.

**Example:** He <u>play**s**</u> road tennis.

✿ **Add 's' to the verbs in brackets and write them in the spaces.**

1. A coconut _____ from the tree. ( fall )

2. The monkey _____ in the tree. ( swing )

3. Every day, Aidan _____. ( read )

4. The factory _____ canes. ( grind )

✿ **Add 's' to these verbs.**

buy _____          make _____

cut _____          give _____

find _____          hear _____

⚘ **Find the verbs in the puzzle.**

```
p   k   t   r   f   b   a   t   s   o
s   x   d   n   e   k   s   e   f   g
a   z   f   g   e   o   i   l   m   i
r   u   n   s   l   w   n   l   b   v
y   b   e   f   s   d   g   s   p   e
l   e   a   r   n   s   s   v   b   s
i   m   t   q   u   w   o   r   k   s
x   d   s   h   t   a   l   k   s   n
r   y   f   w   r   i   t   e   s   v
p   l   a   y   s   m   f   o   r   h
```

| writes | plays | sings | tells |
| eats | feels | runs | works |
| bats | learns | talks | gives |

✤ We add 'ed' to verbs to show action that is finished.

Example:   I <u>walk**ed**</u> home yesterday.

✤ Add 'ed' to the verbs in brackets and write them in the spaces.

1. Yesterday, it _____ all day. ( rain )

2. Last week, Daddy _____ the seeds. ( plant )

3. My cat _____ me last night. ( scratch )

4. This morning, Jan _____ the plants. ( water )

✤ Add 'ed' to these verbs

look _____          smell _____

walk _____          kiss _____

stay _____          push _____

✿ **Circle the verb in each box.**

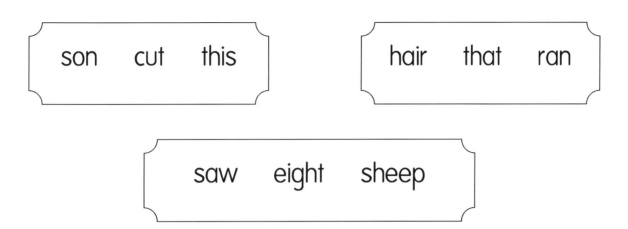

son   cut   this

hair   that   ran

saw   eight   sheep

✿ **Choose a suitable verb to complete the sentences.**

ate    gave    won    sat    wrote

1. The boys _____ many races.

2. I _____ some fish cakes.

3. Uncle _____ me a tablet.

4. They _____ under the big tree.

5. We _____ in our books.

✤ In the boxes, match the present tense to the past tense of the words.

| Present | Past |
|---------|------|
| run | had |
| see | ate |
| eat | saw |
| have | ran |

| Present | Past |
|---------|------|
| get | dug |
| dig | won |
| sit | got |
| win | sat |

✤ Write the correct past tense of the word in the brackets to complete each sentence.

took    hid    fell    told    met

1. The boy _____ off his bike. ( fall )

2. I _____ him at the shop. ( meet )

3. My friend _____ me a secret. ( tell )

4. He _____ a book from the shelf. ( take )

✿ **Circle the verb and write it on the line.**

Example: I (saw) you at the party. <u>saw</u>

1. She looks for the ball. _____

2. He cuts the cake with the girl. _____

3. We pray before lunch. _____

4. He sells snow cones in Bay Street. _____

5. She saved some money. _____

6. They play football on Fridays. _____

7. I picked flowers for my teacher. _____

8. Mummy baked some rock cakes. _____

9. She finds shells on the beach. _____

10. I sat by the window. _____

✿ **Write a suitable verb to complete each sentence.**

1. Cats _____ milk.

2. The dog is _____ at the cat.

3. I like to _____ books.

4. The girl will _____ on the chair.

5. Does Daddy _____ the car?

6. They are _____ to school.

7. Does the sun _____ every day?

8. The girls _____ in the pool.

9. We _____ pizza for lunch.

10. The boys are _____ cricket.

# Section 7

## Adjectives

- Size
- Colour
- Number
- Emotions
- Look / appearance

✤ Words which describe nouns are called adjectives. Match the pictures to the words to describe the size of these nouns.

big

tall

thin

small

short

thick

✿ **Complete the sentences with these 'colour' adjectives to describe the nouns. Colour the pictures.**

| blue | black | white | red | green | yellow |

1. The grass is _____.

2. The sky is _____ and the clouds are

   _____.

3. The apple is _____ but the banana is

   _____.

4. Are her shoes _____?

✿ **Circle the 'colour' adjective in each box.**

| stop    bed    orange |

| cake    brown    tell |

✿ Complete the sentences with these 'number' adjectives to describe the nouns.

| | | | | |
|---|---|---|---|---|
| six | three | four | two | seven |

1. I have _____ eyes.

2. She ate _____ cookies.

3. _____ books are on the shelf.

4. A square has _____ corners.

5. There are _____ days in a week.

Days of the Week
Sunday
Monday
Tuesday
Wednesday
Thursday
Friday
Saturday

✿ Circle the 'number' adjective in each box.

| | | |
|---|---|---|
| flag | one | are |

| | | |
|---|---|---|
| twelve | shoe | were |

✿ Choose an adjective to describe how these people feel.

happy      sad      angry      surprised

1. _____

2. _____

3. _____

4. _____

✿ Choose an adjective from the box to describe these nouns.

hot    soft    sticky    cold    hard    wet

1. _____ ice

2. _____ glue

3. _____ fire

4. _____ cotton

5. _____ rock

6. _____ sponge

✿ **Choose an adjective from the box to describe how these nouns look.**

```
round      curly      fast      big      square

        sharp      tasty      pretty      old
```

_____

_____

_____

_____

_____

_____

_____

_____

_____

❀ **Circle the adjective and write it on the line.**

**Example:** The (little) boy ran home.    little

1. She has long hair. _____

2. Did he win two races? _____

3. The cat caught a fat rat. _____

4. Was the food too hot? _____

5. The blue flag was on the school. _____

6. The angry boy was screaming. _____

7. A yellow bus is parked outside. _____

8. Mummy is wearing a pretty dress. _____

9. May I have a thin slice of bread? _____

10. The pillow is soft. _____

✾ **Write a suitable adjective in each space.**
**Each adjective must be different.**

1. The water is _____.

2. The cat has _____ kittens.

3. That _____ dog bit the man.

4. The man climbs the _____ coconut tree.

5. Does she live in a _____ house?

6. The _____ boy won the race.

7. The _____ girl was crying.

8. The Barbados flag is _____, gold and black.

9. _____ marbles are in the box.

10. Barbados has _____ National Heroes.

# Revision

✿ **Write these nouns in the correct boxes.**

cow    Jack    stove    Oistins    fisherman    library

grass    nurse    horse    watch    sheep    kitchen

Animal

Person

Place

Thing

Make the nouns many and write them in the correct boxes.

| | | | | | |
|---|---|---|---|---|---|
| box | chair | tooth | car | fish | house |
| beach | goose | shoe | die | woman | bus |

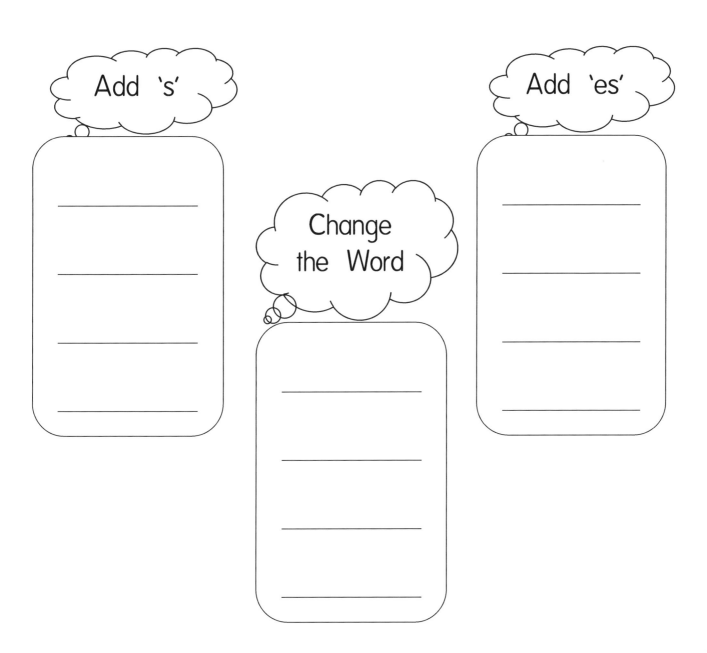

Add 's'

Change the Word

Add 'es'

**✿ Choose words from the box that can be used with the words in the clouds.**

am    is    are    has    have    was    were

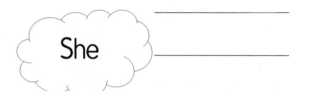

She _____
_____

You _____
_____

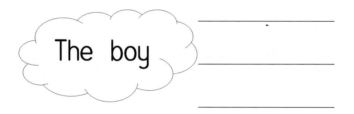

The boy _____
_____

I _____
_____

We _____
_____

✿ Write these special names correctly.

mr. clarke

_____

six roads

_____

november

_____

friday

_____

sunday

_____

april

_____

✿ Write the question words on the lines.

what    come    where    how    they    why    that

_____

_____

_____

_____

✿ **Write the words in the correct boxes.**

| | | | | |
|---|---|---|---|---|
| black | drive | apple | goat | play |
| cold | wide | school | talk | baby |
| swim | happy | chair | clap | eight |

**Nouns**

_____

_____

_____

_____

_____

**Verbs**

_____

_____

_____

_____

_____

**Adjectives**

_____

_____

_____

_____

_____

**Name:** _____

## Grammar Test

A) Write <u>a</u> or <u>an</u> in the correct spaces.

1. _____ table     2. _____ uncle     3. _____ eel

4. We saw _____ bear and _____ alligator at the zoo.

B) Circle the <u>nouns</u> in the sentences.

1. The fishes swim in the water.

2. A cake is on the table.

3. Daddy has a big bag.

*C) Write the correct word from the box in each space.*

```
am        is        are
```

1. She _____ going to the fair.

2. The children _____ playing a game.

3. _____ we going home now?

4. I _____ very happy today.

5. The church _____ open.


*D) Write a <u>full stop</u> or <u>question mark</u> at the end of the sentences.*

1. I have two pencils

2. Did you walk to school

3. What is your sister's name

4. She has a big doll

*E)* *Make the words in brackets mean <u>more than one</u>.*
*Write the answers in the spaces.*

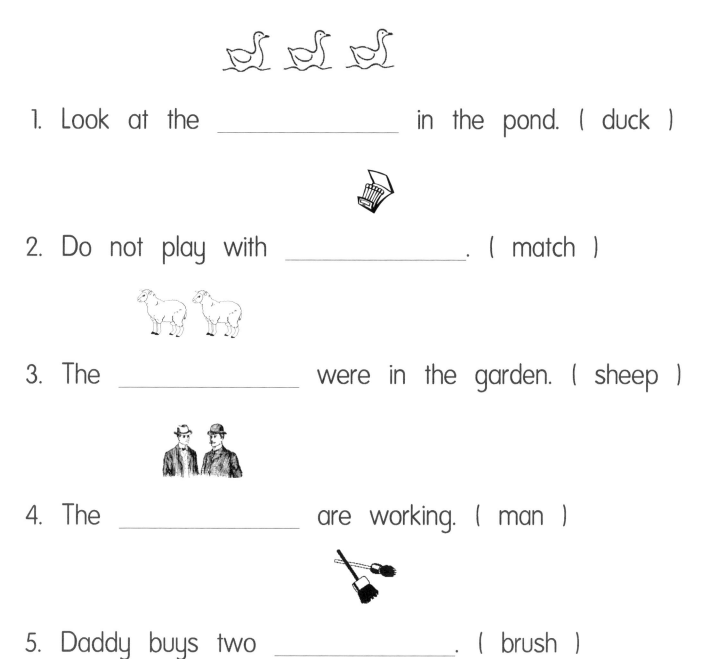

1. Look at the _____ in the pond. ( duck )

2. Do not play with _____. ( match )

3. The _____ were in the garden. ( sheep )

4. The _____ are working. ( man )

5. Daddy buys two _____. ( brush )

## F) Match these words to make compound words.

1.     water          ball

2.     car            cake

3.     foot           fall

4.     cup            ring

5.     ear            pet

## G) Write the correct word from the box in each space.

| was      were |

1. The buses _____ parked.

2. I _____ reading.

3. The book _____ on the table.

4. _____ they eating lunch?

5. Dan and Pam _____ playing.

H) *Underline* the correct word in the brackets.

1. She has ( two  too  to ) books.

2. They play in the ( see  sea ).

3. Daddy puts the ( meat  meet ) on the grill.

4. Look at the pretty ( flour  flower ) in the garden.

5. Mummy buys a ( pear  pair  pare ) of shoes.

I) *Write the correct word from the box in each space.*

```
has          have
```

1. My sister _____ a ball.

2. The rooms _____ not been cleaned.

3. Do you _____ the money?

4. _____ she gone home?

5. We _____ the candles for the cake.

## J) Match each word to its opposite.

1.   right                          dry

2.   wet                           cold

3.   empty                        pull

4.   push                         full

5.   hot                           wrong

## K) Write the <u>opposite</u> of the word in the brackets.

1. The dog ran _____ of the garden. ( in )

2. My _____ brother is four years old. ( big )

3. I have a _____ book. ( old )

4. The _____ girl was laughing. ( sad )

**L)** Circle the <u>verb</u> and write it on the line.

1. The dog jumps up and down. _____

2. The boys played in the sand. _____

3. He ran into the sea. _____

4. The women wash the trays. _____

**M)** Circle the <u>adjective</u> and write it on the line.

1. A black cat is in the tree. _____

2. Is the long pencil yours? _____

3. The girls are angry. _____

4. Two boys were pitching. _____

N) *Rewrite these sentences. Put in capital letters where they are needed.*

1. My birthday is in may.

_____

2. did you walk to school?

_____

3. We are going to bridgetown.

_____

4. On tuesday i am going to the park.

_____

# Homework

| | Page / Pages | | Page / Pages |
|---|---|---|---|
| 1 | | 21 | |
| 2 | | 22 | |
| 3 | | 23 | |
| 4 | | 24 | |
| 5 | | 25 | |
| 6 | | 26 | |
| 7 | | 27 | |
| 8 | | 28 | |
| 9 | | 29 | |
| 10 | | 30 | |
| 11 | | 31 | |
| 12 | | 32 | |
| 13 | | 33 | |
| 14 | | 34 | |
| 15 | | 35 | |
| 16 | | 36 | |
| 17 | | 37 | |
| 18 | | 38 | |
| 19 | | 29 | |
| 20 | | 40 | |

Made in the USA
Columbia, SC
02 September 2024